ABOUT
ENGINEERS

ISAMBARD KINGDOM
BRUNEL

This edition published 2005 by Evans Brothers Limited
2A Portman Mansions
Chiltern Street
London W1U 6NR

British Library Cataloguing in Publication data. A catalogue record for this book is available from the British Library.

Printed in China by WKT Co. Ltd.

ISBN 0237 53077 5

Acknowledgements

The author and publishers would like to thank class Year 4B, St Cuthbert's RC Primary School, Withington, Manchester, for their helpful comments during the making of this book.

For permission to reproduce copyright material, the author and publishers gratefully acknowledge the following:

Cover Firefly leaves Box Tunnel with a Down Express. From the painting by Terence Cuneo O.B.E. The Firefly Trust
Title page The S. S Great Britain, Robert Harding Picture Library
page 5 Bristol City Museum and Art Gallery **page 6** (inset) Hulton Deutsch Collection Limited **page 6-7** Hulton Deutsch Collection Limited **page 8** The Science Museum/Science and Society Picture Library **page 9** Hulton Deutsch Collection Limited **page 10** Mary Evans Picture Library **page 11** Robert Harding Picture Library **page 12** Robert Harding Picture Library **page 13** The Firefly by Terence Cuneo O.B.E, The Firefly Trust **page 14** The Museum of London **page 15** Mary Evans Picture Library **page 16-17** Bristol City Museum and Art Gallery **page 17** (inset) Robert Harding Picture Library **page 18** Mary Evans/Institution of Civil Engineers **page 19** Mary Evans/Institution of Civil Engineers **page 20** Mary Evans Picture Library **page 21** Robert Harding Picture Library

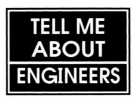

TELL ME ABOUT ENGINEERS

ISAMBARD KINGDOM BRUNEL

written by
John Malam

Evans Brothers Limited

Isambard Kingdom Brunel was born nearly two hundred years ago. He was an engineer and builder. He made bridges, tunnels, ships and even a railway line. People had never seen anything like them before, and they were amazed. Because of all his great works, Isambard became one of the most famous men in Britain. This is his story.

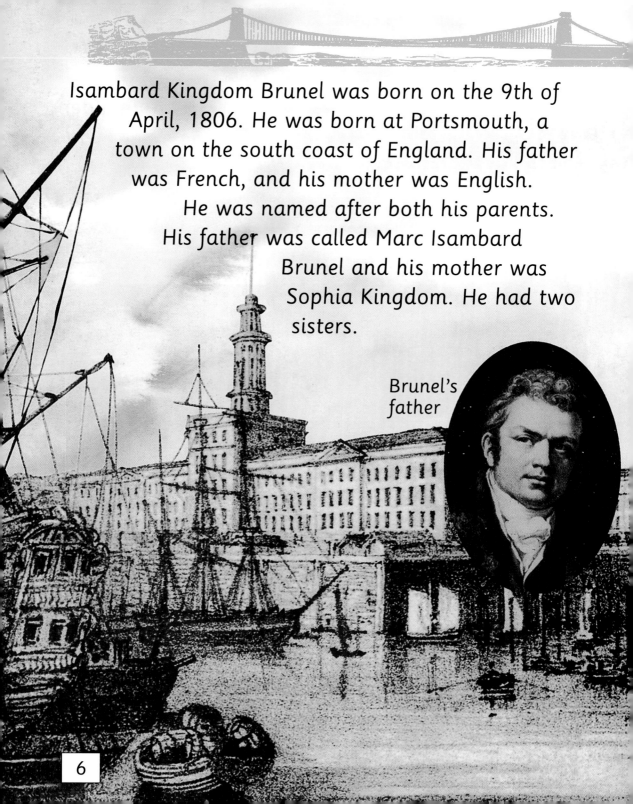

Isambard Kingdom Brunel was born on the 9th of April, 1806. He was born at Portsmouth, a town on the south coast of England. His father was French, and his mother was English.

He was named after both his parents. His father was called Marc Isambard Brunel and his mother was Sophia Kingdom. He had two sisters.

Brunel's father

Isambard's father was a clever man. He was an engineer and an inventor. He wanted his son to become an engineer, too.

When Isambard was six years old, he was taught about geometry. This meant he learned about shapes made from straight lines and curves. This would help him become an engineer.

At first, Isambard went to a boarding school. Then he went to school in France. He learned more about becoming an engineer. When he was sixteen, Isambard came back to England. He began to work for his father, in London.

Portsmouth in Brunel's time

In 1825, Isambard's father began to make a tunnel under the River Thames, in London. The tunnel was called the Thames Tunnel. It was dug by miners. They knew all about digging tunnels.

There were many problems. Isambard's father became ill, and Isambard took over. He was only twenty years old. He worked hard for three years, until his father was well again.

Making the
Thames Tunnel

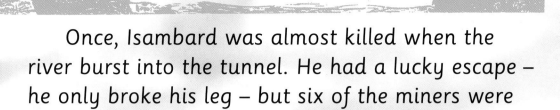

Once, Isambard was almost killed when the river burst into the tunnel. He had a lucky escape – he only broke his leg – but six of the miners were drowned.

It took eighteen years to finish the tunnel. Isambard's father became famous. He was knighted by Queen Victoria. From then on he was called Sir Marc Brunel.

The Thames Tunnel is still used today. Every day, trains carry thousands of people under the River Thames.

The tunnel flooded again and again.

While Isambard's father worked on the Thames Tunnel, Isambard had ideas of his own.

He heard about a competition to make some drawings for a new bridge over the River Avon at Clifton, near Bristol. Isambard made the best drawing and he was asked to build the bridge.

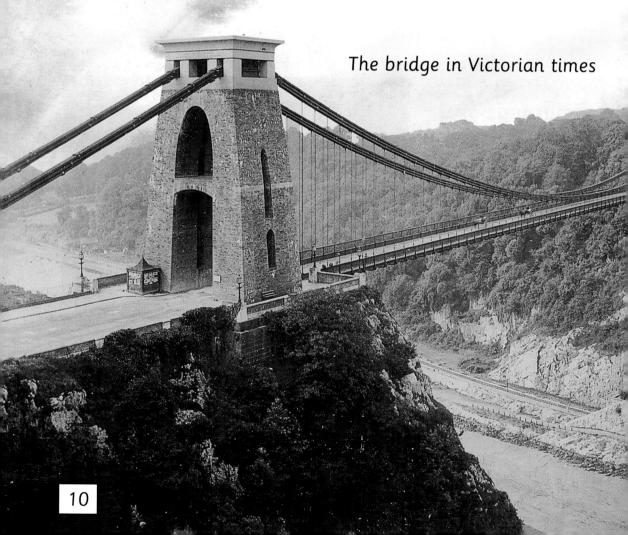

The bridge in Victorian times

In 1831, when he was twenty-five years old, he began to build the Clifton Suspension Bridge. On his bridge the road was suspended, or held up, by iron rods and chains.

It was a long, slow job. It took more than thirty years to build the bridge.

People said the bridge would fall down, but Isambard's famous bridge is still used today.

The bridge today

Isambard lived at an exciting time. Railways were being built between towns. More railways were needed. So Isambard began to build a railway line from London to Bristol. It ran for 190 kilometres (118 miles).

Isambard walked or rode on horseback over every bit of ground from London to Bristol. He did this to work out the best route for the new railway. He hardly stopped for sleep.

Brunel's railway today

Isambard's railway was called the "Great Western Railway". People loved the new railway and it was nicknamed "God's Wonderful Railway". When Queen Victoria travelled on it she became the first British monarch ever to go on a train.

Isambard said his railway was the "finest work in England".

A painting of Brunel's railway

When Isambard was thirty years old, he married Mary Horsley. They had a house in London. Mary liked to ride horses, dress in fine clothes and give parties for all her friends. Isambard and Mary had two sons and a daughter.

London in Brunel's time

Isambard was such a busy man that he spent a lot of time away from his family. In 1838 he even spent Christmas Day in his workshop! He was working on one of his railway engines, trying to make it stronger.

After building his railway, Isambard began to build giant ships. He stayed away from home even more. But all this hard work started to make him ill.

Mary liked to wear clothes like these.

Isambard said he would build giant ships to take people from England to America.

His first ship was called the "Great Western". It was a steamship. On its first voyage an accident happened. The wooden ship caught fire. Isambard tried to put it out but he slipped and fell. For the second time in his life he was almost killed.

When the fire was out, the "Great Western" sailed to New York, in America, without Isambard. He stayed in England to get well again.

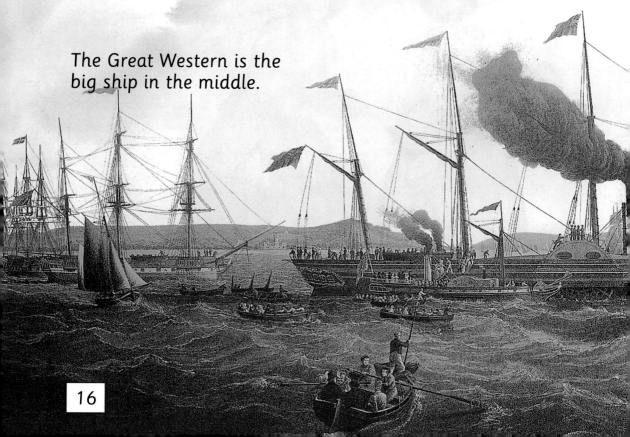

The Great Western is the big ship in the middle.

Isambard said his next ship would be bigger than the "Great Western" and he would make it from sheets of iron. People said it could not be done. But Isambard had made up his mind. He called this ship the "Great Britain".

The "Great Britain" took people to America and Australia. When it grew old, it carried coal. It sailed more than one million miles.

You can visit the Great Britain in Bristol.

Isambard built one more ship. He called it the "Great Eastern". It was twice as big as the "Great Britain"! It was the biggest ship in the world.

Brunel is standing in front of the chains used to launch the Great Eastern.

Thousands of people watched as the "Great Eastern" was launched. It was so big it had to be launched sideways. But when the time came, it hardly moved at all. Isambard's giant ship was stuck. It took several more goes, using stronger and stronger machines, to push the ship into the water.

The Great Eastern being built

After the launch there was still much to do before the ship was ready. Sadly, Isambard never lived to see his last great ship sail around the world. He grew ill. All his years of hard, dangerous work had made him weak. His doctor said he needed to rest in a warm country. He went to Egypt with his family, where he saw the pyramids.

Not long after he came back from Egypt he fell ill again. On the 15th of September, 1859, he died. He was fifty-three years old.

The pyramids in Egypt in Brunel's time

Important dates

1806 Brunel was born
1820 He went to school in France
1822 He started to work for his father
1827 He became the chief engineer on the Thames
         Tunnel
1828 He broke his leg in an accident inside the
         Thames Tunnel
1831 He started to build the Clifton Suspension
         Bridge
1835 He started to build the
         Great Western Railway
1836 He married Mary Horsley
1837 The "Great Western" ship
         was launched
1837 He almost died in a fire
         on the "Great Western"
1843 The "Great Britain" ship
         was launched
1858 The "Great Eastern" ship
         was launched
1859 Brunel died

A statue of Isambard Kingdom Brunel
at Paddington railway station, London.

21

Keywords

engineer
someone who works out how to make bridges, railways, ships and large buildings

geometry
a subject all about shapes made from straight lines, curves and angles

miner
someone who works under the ground

monarch
a ruler of a country such as a king or queen

steamship
a ship driven by steam. Steam turns paddle wheels round. As the wheels turn in the water, the ship moves forward.

suspension bridge
a bridge where the road is held up by strong wires

Index